THE DEBT-FREE COLLEGE ATHLETE

RYAN DAVIS

WESTBOW
PRESS®
A DIVISION OF THOMAS NELSON
& ZONDERVAN

WestBow Press books may be ordered through booksellers or by contacting:

WestBow Press
A Division of Thomas Nelson & Zondervan
1663 Liberty Drive
Bloomington, IN 47403
www.westbowpress.com
1 (866) 928-1240

ISBN: 978-1-5127-2334-2 (sc)
ISBN: 978-1-5127-2335-9 (hc)
ISBN: 978-1-5127-2333-5 (e)

Library of Congress Control Number: 2015920516

Print information available on the last page.

WestBow Press rev. date: 1/29/2016

CONTENTS

Dedicated to my parents,
who gave me everything I needed to succeed in life
and led me to the fountain of living waters.

INTRODUCTION

We're going to be a little unconventional.

In my years of mentoring and training athletes, the traditional approach works in most situations. It works when there's enough time, enough resources, enough experience to accomplish the goal.

But when we don't have one (or any) of those, then it's time for a different game plan. In tough situations, we've got to be unconventional.

The equivalent in the game of being a Debt-Free College Athlete is that, traditionally I could give you some financial know-how, a rundown of how college works, and leave you with a to-do list. That would be the case if being a DFCA were a cake-walk.

But it's not.

It's quite a feat. But it's all good, because over the years I have learned the unconventional playbook — and it works.

And it worked for James too ...

I pressed the start button on the treadmill to begin the 12-minute fitness test. James began sucking wind around five minutes and reached his physical limit just two minutes later. Dripping with sweat, he was huffing and puffing with a flushed white face. He stumbled off the treadmill to the bathroom and quickly threw up.

This was bad news.

James was determined to be a Division I athlete, and I was hired to train him to get there. The problem was, he only had one month before tryouts and he was unable to do a baseline fitness test.

When I first started working with him, just 7 months before tryouts, I knew from watching his technique and form that we were going to need a miracle. He was extremely tense, choppy, mentally defeated, and physically beat-up.

To make matters worse, James had several recurring injuries, some of which had been operated on. A few meaning; knee, back, hip, groin, and ankle — it was rough.

His knee surgery impacted the muscle mass in his leg so that one leg was larger and stronger than the other, and he was unable to balance them out since the surgery. Before each training session he would wrap his ankle tight to avoid rolling it again, and he put on a heavy groin wrap to avoid pulling that again. He often looked like he was prepared for battle by the time we were ready to begin training.

James was also emotionally in a tough place. He had very little confidence and what confidence he had seemed easily shakable.

Every time he would fall short even a bit, it would wreck him mentally.

I came to find that James was consistently overtraining and wouldn't rest. His mom would find him training late at night in the basement trying to improve his skills. James' insatiable desire to improve his game was eating up his rest time and testing his recurring injuries.

After our first training session, I felt terrible. I wasn't sure I could help him become a D1 soccer player even if we had 2+ years to work together. I had recently graduated college as a D1 soccer player so I knew what it took to play at that level. I could tell he was a very long way away, and time was not on his side with just 7 months until he needed to be ready.

In the beginning, we were working together only once a week for an hour, the traditional approach.

However, I knew if he was even going to have a shot at his dreams, we would have to get serious and unconventional.

I called James' mom with a proposition. First of all, it was clear to me we needed to train five times a week if James was going to be able to have a chance.

But I also knew that physical and sport-specific training wasn't going to be enough. If James didn't improve his perspective, he wouldn't make it to the finish.

I proposed two hours each practice. The first portion (30-45 minutes) would be spiritual and mental conditioning. The second portion would be sport-specific training.

I knew this wouldn't sit well with James, but I knew we couldn't climb this mountain on foot. We needed a helicopter mindset to fly over it. What transpired was crazy.

Every day for 7 months, we would read a portion of the gospels from the Bible and talk through the scriptures, eliminating toxic thinking and replacing it with truth.

Fast-forward six months to our treadmill incident with just one month before tryouts. Only *one week* after his incident from the treadmill test, James learned how to 'pray in the spirit' and tried it out while running the speed test again.

Five minutes passed, and he had no sign of fatigue. Seven minutes passed and he was running steady. Nine minutes passed and he was sweating but going strong. Finally he hit the 12-minute mark and got off the treadmill in shock. He was hardly even tired!

We hugged each other out of excitement. In just one week, the impossible had become possible. He had experienced approximately a 40% increase in his cardiovascular endurance without any changes in diet or training. Gains like this would conventionally take a minimum of 2 to 4 months with vigorous workouts and focus on fitness.

Another time, his recurring hip injury healed completely overnight, after his mom prayed for the fear in his life to be gone.

We saw James transform from a below average player into a D1 athlete with unconventional approach. With God at the center of his training, the sky was the limit.

This unconventional approach proved that it's not always hard work that helps us win. It's letting God in the picture.

With God in the picture, the impossible becomes possible, and it's why we need to start with the spiritual and follow up with the tactical. As we combine the two, we will experience amazing victory, just like my young friend did.

And what about James now? Well he's not playing Division I soccer. He turned down a D1 college offer to play soccer professionally in a foreign country. It's safe to say he's living his dreams.

I'm going to take you on a journey in this book like I did with James. I'm going to share the spiritual side of the picture first to get us mentally in the place we need to be. We'll build truth in our thinking and let God into the picture to cultivate an environment for the impossible to become possible.

Then we're going to get into some of the details of how to carry this out and become a debt-free college athlete no matter where you decide to go to school.

My goal is to shed light on this entire college process as a student athlete so you can come out on top in the end. I believe if you follow through on the items in this book you'll see results that will inspire you and build your trust in God as you see the impossible come to pass. I'm thrilled to hear your victory story when it's all said and done.

Expect great things.

Here we go!

CHAPTER 1

THE JOURNEY BEGINS

I remember being in your place just a few years ago. I remember wondering where I was going to go to school, who I would play for, and ultimately questioning how I was going to pull it off financially.

Searching for colleges is an exciting time of life but I know it can be dampened by the mountain-sized financial obstacles, standing between you and the college experience of your dreams.

The many parents and student athletes I speak with today are in the exact same boat. They want to know what to expect throughout this process. They crave more knowledge. They want to know how to choose the best college or university and they want to know they're on the right track, doing the right things to give their son or daughter the best college experience possible.

Well, hindsight is 20/20, and I'm excited that you chose to invest in this book for wisdom on the collegiate selection process and paying for it without the help of student loans. By the end of our time together I know you'll have a much clearer picture of how you can have an amazing college tenure and do it completely debt-free.

When I began my college search I didn't have too much going for me from an outsider's perspective. Both of my parents were making very modest salaries as full-time ministers and although I was having a successful student athlete tenure in high school, I wasn't necessarily the next Pelé on the soccer field or the next Einstein in the classroom according to my first score on the SAT.

To make matters more interesting, my parents told me from the very beginning of my college search that neither they nor I would be taking out *any* student loans to pay for college.

So there I had it. If I was going to have a higher education, I was going to have to get it fully funded by way of athletic or academic scholarships and grants (money that I wouldn't have to borrow or pay back). As you can imagine this made things very interesting for me but looking back I wouldn't have had it any other way. Approaching college this way practically forced me to trust God to provide for my needs and I wouldn't trade that adventure for anything. My post-college life has been shaped by these experiences. Seeing God come through for me over and over again in college has allowed me to live without fear after college when challenges in life arise. I've come to realize that God is real,

He is on my side and when I partner with Him there's nothing I can't do.

Knowing God will always come through for us eliminates fear from our lives and replaces it with power, love and a sound thinking. If we can learn to lean on God now we set ourselves up for an amazing life in the future. Allowing God to provide for our higher education just happens to be a great time to learn these lessons.

I'm excited for all the young people who read this book because I know as you place your trust in God and do your best, you will graduate from college with loads of miracle stories, priceless memories and great honors from your journey. You can have a spectacular college experience that exceeds your expectations and you can do it completely debt-free. Taking the unconventional route will get you there.

CHAPTER 2

THE CHALLENGE

Today nearly everyone is trying to find ways to afford college. With the rising prices for tuition rates, out-of-state fees, books, room, board, and other costs, most families can't keep up with the bills on their own. With this pressure to pay for college, parents and student athletes are seeing no other way to afford college but by borrowing money from outside sources.

I had a friend in high school who was a fantastic soccer player and student. He came to practice one day on cloud nine with news that he'd gotten recruited to play at one of the best schools in the country for soccer. We were all stunned and jealous.

It really seemed like a dream opportunity. He even said it was all paid for, out-of-state tuition and everything! However, it turns out

FASFA was the one who fronted the bill in the form of student loans. The real price to attend this university and come off the bench for four years was a crippling load of debt to the tune of $50,000.

Some refer to student loans as an investment toward a bright future. A college education, however, is a very liquid investment, one where many factors may alter the outcome.

For instance, a young man I knew was proudly accepted at Yale his senior year of high school. His parents weren't poor but they weren't rich either. After finishing out his college tenure he had racked up over $60,000 in student loan debt with the high tuition and fees at the prestigious university.

I'm sure as a senior in high school he assumed that with a degree from Yale he would certainly have a job that would pay back any loans he had in a very short period of time. After graduation, however, he decided to follow his newly found passion and he became a gardener in Italy. What a fun dream! But I'd wager a pretty penny he wishes he had financial freedom in Italy while pursuing his dream.

As a high school student athlete it's exciting to receive seemingly easy money to get you where you want to go. The fact of the matter is that this easy money offered from the government, colleges and banks have hooks attached to them that require years of commitment and interest in order to pay back. Although student loans seem to provide great freedom at first glance, they end up creating great financial and mental burdens to the borrower after college.

I've seen too many incredible young adults drown in their debt. They graduate with hope, great aspiration and big dreams only to sink under the weight of their acquired debt. Their dreams become too far out of reach and they begin to settle for mediocrity as the pressure for money increases. Life after college ends up becoming a stressful time to search for work and pay off loan sharks knocking at the door, rather than a free time to pursue their calling.

I also know a young woman who is an amazing writer and artist. She's a bright woman all around and has the motivation and desire to affect young people's lives in a very powerful way. However, after a couple months of job searching after graduating she came face to face with her dues.

Because she needed to earn money fast to pay off her student loans, she reluctantly settled for a career in business banking - something she never really desired. Although she was upset with her decision, she said it had to happen in order to pay her bills and her student loans. Taking the job was the only way to stop her from sinking.

This young woman now sees herself staying in this field of business banking for the remainder of her career because of the financial security it provides for her. She went into college and graduated with a drive to meet her calling but her student loans were simply too heavy to stay afloat. She said it herself, that it doesn't take long after graduating with student loan debt to lose sight of your dreams and settle for less than what you want.

My wife Stephanie had similar ability and ambition and graduated without student loan debt. Because of this she was able to wait out the job hunt and founded her own branding and marketing company that blossomed. Without the pressure and burden of student loans she was able to do what she loved and felt called to do.

Today nearly *seventy percent* of all college students are borrowing money in an attempt to sweep the bill under the rug for their college education. The average college student will graduate with a bachelor's degree owing nearly $28,000 in student loan debt and 1 out of every 8 borrowers will graduate with over $50,000 in student loan debt.

Based on these statistics, let's ask ourselves a question as followers of Jesus Christ. Just because the average person is borrowing money for school does that mean that we as Christians should do the same? I would suggest the opposite! We are far from average.

We are God's masterpieces (Ephesians 2:10), we are children of the Most High God — royalty in Christ Jesus (I Peter 2:9), God lives in us (I Corinthians 3:16)! It seems we are the polar opposite of average.

So these average statistics should immediately raise a red flag in our minds. They should help us recognize that the average route is likely not the route for us as extraordinary children of God.

God has called us to live as examples to the world. This includes being examples in our financial decisions to trust God to provide for our college education.

From the world's perspective it may seem like there's no way to have the college experience we desire without borrowing money to do it, but I can assure you there is. It's through Jesus Christ, the way, the truth and the life that we discover the more abundant life before, during and after college. He provides a better way.

CHAPTER 3

A BETTER WAY

While developing as a soccer player, I was taught how to kick a soccer ball. At the time, I was using the very tip of my toe to kick the ball. It seemed effective, and I became convinced that it was the best way to kick because I could actually get the ball to soar in the air.

Then one day, my coach taught me a better way to strike a soccer ball. He showed me the many different areas of the foot that I could strike the ball so I could be more successful as a soccer player.

At first I didn't believe what he was saying. I didn't think there could be a better way to kick a soccer ball. I *knew* what worked, and what worked was kicking the soccer ball with my toe, not the places he taught me. But as I continued to practice what he taught me and trusted his advice, I was able to learn how to manipulate, pass, and shoot the ball in ways I had never imagined.

In the same way, God has given us His wisdom for our lives by way of His Word. In His Word, He instructs us on ways we can take a higher and better route in life. Although we may be set in our ways and believe we know what's good, God shows us the best way to live in order to have abundance in all areas of our lives. Father knows best.

God wants us to prove Him in our lives. He wants us to run to Him so He can supply all our needs. Just like our earthly fathers' natural desire to provide for our every need, our heavenly Father desires to provide for us in an unforgettable, supernatural fashion. However, when we don't turn to Him, we find ourselves making the same mistakes God's children made several thousand years ago. We can learn about this in Jeremiah 2:13: "For my people have committed two evils, they have forsaken Me, the fountain of living waters and hewn them out cisterns, broken cisterns that can hold no water" (KJV).

This point tends to be a central issue if we experience lack. We may be forsaking God, the fountain of living waters, for our own cracked water bottles.

Forsaking God means abandoning Him. Instead of claiming God's blessings and allowing Him to meet our needs, we oftentimes unknowingly abandon Him and try to provide for ourselves instead.

When we don't run to God and rest in His strength, it's easy to become fearful. Without Him, we must always keep moving, looking for more resources. We make cisterns, or smaller containers, for ourselves, but they are *never* enough. The cisterns we make are always cracked and leaking, and we're found always needing more.

As we continue to move ahead with our eyes fixed on solving our problems on our own, we finally get to a point where we find the resources we need. But this time, we don't find them at the fountain of living waters; we abandoned that a long time ago. We find them elsewhere in the world. We begin to see the vast resources and riches the world can provide. It now becomes our hope to get our needs met. We're thirsty and in need, so we decide to take from these outside resources and our cisterns finally get filled. Praise God, right! Right? Oh, right—God …

> Hey, God! Guess what? I'm getting my needs met now. Everything is turning out okay! Don't worry; I still want to be your friend, but as far as my needs and resources go, I'm going let the world take care of those. But we can have a great long-distance relationship! I just don't really want to rely on You to provide for my needs.

We fill up our cisterns and make even bigger ones to fill. They hold more water initially, but the same truth applies. Our cisterns leak and *hold no water*. No matter how grand our cisterns may be, they leak, and we will always be left needing more.

If we're going to have our needs met and the desires of our hearts supplied, then we need to go to the lasting source of fulfillment and supply, the fountain of living waters—our heavenly Father, God. He has all the resources in the universe at His disposal. He is simply waiting for us to come to Him and trust Him so He as our Father can supply all our needs.

CHAPTER 4

A FORK IN THE ROAD

After I learned the fundamentals of soccer, I became quite skilled at the sport. There came a point in my career where college coaches began to attend our soccer games.

One particular game when a coach came to watch me play, I wanted to do everything I could to impress him. In the first half, I did things simply to showcase my skill. At halftime I received a talking to from my coach, because I was risking the result of the game to showcase my individual skill as a soccer player. I was serving myself, not the team.

When I was reminded at halftime that we were competing in this game *together* to win *together*, I really thought about my intentions on the field. I had a decision to make—whether to serve myself, or the team. I realized that if I wanted to win, I had to make the decision to serve my team rather than myself (which made me a better player in return). I realized that I couldn't play for myself, and my own glory, and play for my team at the same time. I had to choose one or the other.

In the same way, throughout our lives we will also have the choice to serve two entities—God or money. Jesus teaches this in Matthew 6:24: "No one can serve two masters. Either you will hate the one and love the other, or you will be devoted to the one and despise the other. You cannot serve both God and money" (NIV).

We can only serve one master, and God gave us free will to decide whom we want to serve. The choices are clear: God or money. Which one we decide to serve will dramatically shape the course of our lives. So do we want to serve God or money?

Although the answer may seem obvious to most Christians, it is an important question for us to get a clear, definitive answer to. I have seen many Christians, including myself, fall prey to serving money. Although it may seem we are serving God, our thoughts, words, and actions reflect our allegiance to the dollar.

Some signposts that we are serving money may come in the form of limiting ourselves to our current financial situations, dreaming small, living and operating within our comfort zones to avoid risk, and the big one I see most often, lack of tithing, which we will touch on in more detail shortly.

"Whom will we serve?" is a pivotal question for all of us. Let's challenge ourselves now to take an honest look at our hearts and decide on a clear answer. I believe if we do this now, we won't waver when we are challenged in the future.

If we are going to serve either God or money, we may want to figure out what it means to be a servant. Wisdom from Proverbs sheds some light on this for us: "The borrower is servant to the lender" (Proverbs 22:7b KJV).

As we study the word "servant" in this passage, we begin to get a better picture of what it means. This word paints a picture of someone who subjects himself or herself to work for another.

When we borrow money, we make the decision to subject ourselves to work for the lender. If we decide to borrow money from an institution, then we become servants to it. This makes sense practically, as we borrow money from the institution and are obligated to pay it back with interest over time.

As we borrow money from the world, we begin to work for these organizations. We spend our time serving them from the moment we borrow until our bills and interest are paid off in full.

We must recognize that whomever we decide to borrow from, we will serve. If we choose to borrow money from organizations in the world, we will serve them with our time, energy, money, and many years of our lives. In choosing to serve money, we willingly subject ourselves to work for those who lend us money.

However, even the world is beginning to recognize the downfall of borrowing money for college. While passing through an airport in Florida, I stopped to read the bold front page headline of *USA Today:* "1.1 trillion Millennials' ball-and-chain: Student loan debt." The article went on to explain how many graduates in their twenties and thirties are still paying off student loans, delaying their dreams of marrying, buying a home, and starting their families.

Dallas Mavericks owner and billionaire entrepreneur Mark Cuban has much to say on the topic of student loans and how they are crippling the economy. In May of 2014, Mark shared his thoughts on student loans at *Inc.'s* 17th annual GROWCO conference in Nashville Tennessee,

> If Mark Cuban is running the economy, I'd go and say, "Sallie Mae, the maximum amount you're allowed to guarantee for any student in a year is $10,000, period, end of story."

> We can talk about Republican or Democrat approaches to the economy, but until you fix the student loan bubble—and that's where the real bubble is—we don't have a chance. All this other stuff is shuffling deck chairs on the Titanic.

Because college grads graduate with a deficit, they have no money to spend, and it's clogging the prosperity of a nation and stealing our freedom.

Because God's heart is to always give us freedom and because we know that where the spirit of the Lord is there is freedom (2 Corinthians 3:17) it is clear that the method of borrowing money to pay for a higher education is not something that God directs us to. The only thing God desires us to owe others is found in the book of Romans:

"Owe no man any thing, but to love one another: For he that loveth another hath fulfilled the law" (Romans 13:8 KJV).

Love is what we owe others. In loving others we fulfill the law and the new command Jesus gave to us to love others the way He loved us (John 13:34). The great debt we have to man is not financial, it's to love them like Jesus loved us.

Before we close this section I want to direct our attention to the context of Matthew 6:24. It's interesting to note that the context surrounding this scripture where Jesus states, "...You cannot serve both God and money" is centered on God's provision for our lives.

Let's read this passage together to better digest Jesus' point to us about what God's provision looks like:

> Do not store up for yourselves treasures on earth, where moths and vermin destroy, and where thieves break in and steal. But store up for yourselves treasures in heaven, where moths and vermin do not destroy, and where thieves do not break in and steal. For where your treasure is, there your heart will be also.
>
> The eye is the lamp of the body. If your eyes are healthy, your whole body will be full of light. But if your eyes are unhealthy, your whole body will be full of darkness. If then the light within you is darkness, how great is that darkness!
>
> No one can serve two masters. Either you will hate the one and love the other, or you will be devoted to the one and despise the other. You cannot serve both God and money.

Therefore I tell you, do not worry about your life, what you will eat or drink; or about your body, what you will wear. Is not life more than food, and the body more than clothes?

Look at the birds of the air; they do not sow or reap or store away in barns, and yet your heavenly Father feeds them. Are you not much more valuable than they?

Can any one of you by worrying add a single hour to your life?

And why do you worry about clothes? See how the flowers of the field grow. They do not labor or spin.

Yet I tell you that not even Solomon in all his splendor was dressed like one of these.

If that is how God clothes the grass of the field, which is here today and tomorrow is thrown into the fire, will he not much more clothe you—you of little faith?

So do not worry, saying, 'What shall we eat?' or 'What shall we drink?' or 'What shall we wear?' For the pagans run after all these things, and your heavenly Father knows that you need them.

But seek first his kingdom and his righteousness, and all these things will be given to you as well.

Therefore do not worry about tomorrow, for tomorrow will worry about itself. Each day has enough trouble of its own (Matthew 6:19-34 NIV).

God's provision for us and our children is complete. As we seek God's kingdom and His righteousness first, God gives us all that we will ever need in a glorious fashion.

It's important for parents to recognize that as much as we would love to keep our kids safe in the comfort of our provision we must allow God to be their number one protector and provider. Training our children to understand the strength of their heavenly Father is priceless as they grow into adulthood. It's *now* that you can help them set a tone and pattern for how they will make decisions when they are out of the house.

If we teach them to serve money by relying on the student loans to get them what they want, then a standard is set for them to go to the world to get their needs met. If we challenge our children and ourselves to allow God to show us His love and power to provide for all we need for college finances, we set a tone and standard for our children to go to God for love, answers, and to get their needs met.

Parents, the time is *now* to show your children just how much their Heavenly Father loves them. Let's train and lead them to go to God for all the answers of life and raise up a new generation of deep-rooted believers who love and trust God like never before. I believe in doing this we will lead the next generation to trust in God for supernatural and miraculous results that only our God could bring.

This leads us to our other option of service — God. We can choose to love and serve God rather than money.

But what does serving God look like? Is serving God something that we really want to do? Is serving Him truly the better way?

Many amazing men and women in the New Testament referred to themselves as servants of God and our Lord Jesus Christ. Some include Mary (the mother of Jesus), Paul, Peter, Jude and James. Why would they want to serve God and our Lord Jesus Christ over money? Let's take a look at the book of James to understand why they would make this choice: "James a servant of God and of the Lord Jesus Christ, to the twelve tribes scattered among the nations: greetings" (James 1:1 NIV).

The word servant in this verse is the Greek word *doulos*. This word carries an amazing story with it.

In Bible times, a person who simply worked as a servant was not called a *doulos*. A person was called a *doulos* after they served their master for seven years and were then given the opportunity to be set free from their servitude, and in the end decided to stay with their master.

The motivation for the servant to stay was out of a love for their master. If the servant loved their master and decided to stay they would pierce their ear as a sign they were a *doulos* to their master. At this point they became an addition to the family and were treated as such. A *doulos* was even given a signet ring of the master he willingly served to make important business dealings on behalf of his master. A *doulos* was part of the family.

What does this mean for us if we decide we want to serve God over money?

Wherefore thou art no more a servant, but a son; and if a son, then an heir of God through Christ (Galatians 4:7 KJV).

The Spirit itself beareth witness with our spirit, that we are the children of God: And if children, then heirs; heirs of God, and joint-heirs with Christ (Romans 8:16-17a KJV).

For he that is called in the Lord, being a servant, is the Lord's freeman: likewise also he that is called, being free, is Christ's servant. Ye are bought with a price; be not ye the servants of men (I Corinthians 7:22-23 KJV).

Ladies and gentlemen what a God we have the opportunity to serve! You see, when we get born again we become God's sons and daughters. We become a part of God's royal family and become heirs of God and joint-heirs of God's inheritance with Jesus Christ! It's from our place of sonship that we can decide we want to serve our Heavenly Father and our Lord Jesus Christ.

I believe this is why the many amazing believers like Mary, Paul, Peter, Timothy, Jude and others referred to themselves as *doulos*. They wanted to serve God out of thankfulness for their sonship. They weren't obligated to serve God but they made the decision to because they loved Him so.

God desires our relationship as His children. He wants to love us and give us richly all things to enjoy. We become His servants or *doulos* as we willingly choose to serve Him out of our thankfulness for our sonship! We serve a loving Heavenly Father and a wonderful Lord. We are adopted into the royal family! It's out of this love for God that we decide to serve Him.

21

What is different about serving God is that as we choose to love and serve Him we experience the highest form of freedom. As God's kids we have a great inheritance to enjoy. We can ask Him for anything according to His Word and He hears us.

If we want to experience the supernatural favor of God it's important we choose to serve God, not money, and simply taking part in the inheritance we have as God's children. God loves us and He will meet our need. He wants to be our source of unlimited supply if we will only let Him.

Serving money and borrowing it requires us to work harder and harder to supply for ourselves because our source of supply is always leaking. When this happens we become quickly overworked and in the end find ourselves abandoning God. When we decide to serve money by means of borrowing it, we will have great need because our cisterns are broken and can hold no water.

But as God's kids, we can choose to serve God out of our love for Him. We recognize that He is our provider, our fountain of unlimited supply and we can rest assured that He will exceed our expectations in every way as we turn to Him, rely on Him and trust in Him.

Now the rubber meets the road. Let's prove that this stuff we're learning actually works. I'll start by showing you how God came through for me personally. In doing so I hope to give you a glimpse of how He will come through for you as you place your trust in Him.

CHAPTER 5

PROVE IT

Although I had my first two years at community college completely paid for through athletic and academic scholarships, it came time to transfer to the big Division I soccer fields and campuses. At this point, I felt like small fish, trying to compete for attention and funding, in a big sea. It was evident that I could no longer provide for myself on my own ability and merit any longer.

The school of my dreams, Bowling Green State University, was $30,000 per year out of my reach, and a $60,000 tab was not something my family or I could afford to pay.

At this point I was still considered an out-of-state resident, I didn't receive *one* award letter for scholarships or grants I had applied to, and to top it off I wasn't receiving much interest from the BGSU coach either.

Although I had always been taught to do my best and let God do the rest, I knew I was doing all that I could and more. I was saving every penny that I could. I was looking into every avenue possible to receive financial aid for my final two years of schooling, but nothing and I mean *nothing* was coming through.

Time kept on ticking and my doom seemed to be more of a reality with each day that passed. God seemed so distant. I began to think it was now too late for God to swing into the rescue for me.

In the midst of my impending doom I received a pivotal e-mail from my girlfriend's father (who is now my father-in-law). Within his email lay the missing key to unlock the doors of God's prosperity for me. He reminded me to do one thing — *tithe.*

Tithing is a biblical principal practiced in the Old and New Testaments. The term tithe means a tenth. Tithing refers to giving ten percent of our net earnings to God.

Tithing is a principal that helps us remember God is our source of unlimited supply. It's a practice that brings our focus and reliance back to God, the fountain of living waters.

When I was reminded about tithing, I remembered a passage of scripture that paints a vivid picture of the abundance God provides as I acknowledge Him with my finances. We can see this in Malachi 3:10:

> Bring ye all the tithes into the storehouse, that there may be meat in mine house, and prove me now herewith, saith the Lord of hosts, if I will not open you

the windows of heaven, and pour you out a blessing, that there shall not be room enough to receive it (Malachi 3:10 KJV).

What a beautiful promise to know! As I prove God by tithing, God opens up the windows of heaven and pours out a blessing that I won't have room enough to receive all of it!

When we tithe we are proving God. We give Him what many people in the world serve, money, and He opens up a whole new world to us — a world filled with His supernatural provision.

The question for me at this point was, how could I give away ten percent of my paycheck when I was already struggling to save money for college? I was trying to save my money to pay for school, not put another dent in my paycheck. I simply felt like I couldn't afford to give up ten percent of my earnings to God. But the real question for me at that point was, could I afford not to?

> But this I say, He which soweth sparingly shall reap also sparingly; and he which soweth bountifully shall reap also bountifully. Every man according as he purposeth in his heart, so let him give; not grudgingly, or of necessity: for God loveth a cheerful giver. And God is able to make all grace abound toward you; that ye, always having all sufficiency in all things, may abound to every good work (II Corinthians 9:6-9 KJV).

I needed a bountiful harvest of finances to get into Bowling Green. I began to realize that I needed to do my part to prove God and tithe, and allow God to do His part and open up the windows of heaven for me.

I tithed that week and for the first time in a long time. It was here that I knew I had honestly put my trust in God to meet my needs for college.

Now God was in the limelight. Now He was up to bat and I needed a home run.

The same day that I tithed, the leader of our campus Bible fellowship gave me the name of someone she respected and trusted in student aid services at BGSU. This man had worked with some of the other kids who had attended the campus Bible fellowship, and helped them find ways to finance their education. That very day I called his office and scheduled an appointment to speak with him in person the following day.

When I entered his office, we greeted each other, sat down, and before we began he showed me the several thank you cards he had held on to from the past students who had shown their gratitude for his help that were a part of the same campus Bible fellowship. "Look here Ryan, I still have all the thank you cards from those wonderful kids. What a great bunch. Ryan, what can I do for you?" he said enthusiastically.

I began to tell him about my $60,000 predicament and showed him the ways I was trying to earn the finances to attend BGSU that upcoming fall. I then showed him the student athlete profile I compiled, which showcased some of my accomplishments in academia, extracurricular and athletics. "We have to have something here for you. There just has to be something," he said as he got up from his chair and began to exit the room.

I waited for about five minutes in his office, somewhat confused, wondering what he was doing exactly.

As it turns out, he was going to each and every scholarship coordinator he knew, asking them personally if I would be eligible for any of their awards.

He came back into the office with a middle-aged woman who looked like she knew her stuff. She wasted no time to show me the inside of a flimsy single-page pamphlet and said, "Hi Ryan. I'm sorry but there are only two scholarships that we have for transfer students at this University."

So, I asked how much they were worth and she said, "One thousand per scholarship."

Needless to say, I was deflated. At that moment, my bill for next year was $30,000 and the only two scholarships I could apply for combined to a wimpy total of just $2,000.

As I looked away from her, eyes to the floor, trying to mask my defeated soul, she said, "So the only thing I can do for you, is award you the Excellence Grant and hope for the best from there."

I paused for a moment and thought about what she said, slowly realizing that she just told me she was going to *give* me a grant. I asked to clarify, "Did you just say you were going to give me a grant?"

She replied calmly and matter-of-factly, "Yes."

I was freaking out inside! "How much is the grant for?" I asked.

"Two thousand dollars. If I could just have you sign here we'll apply it to your account today," she replied in her run-of-the-mill tone once again.

I couldn't hold it in! This phantom woman had just given me $2,000 in grant aid at the drop of a dime! I smiled so big she could see my wisdom teeth and I asked, "Can I hug you?!"

She smiled and we embraced. I read the fine print and simply signed my name to receive a $2,000 grant.

I gave both administrators a huge hug before I left, while thanking them for everything they had just done for me.

I left that room *on fire*. I immediately called my girlfriend's father and told him how I took heed to his e-mail and began to prove God and trust Him by tithing. I talked his ear off about the concrete results I had seen from God in just one day with the $2,000 grant. He was ecstatic and said,

> "Ryan, if God is real and is true to His Word, and I believe He is, you'll receive everything you need to go to college at Bowling Green. He promises He will supply all our need as we seek Him first. You chose this University because you decided to give God first place in your life. He is going to provide for you just like He promised."

I was pretty excited about seeing God go to work for me but I still had a long way to go — $58,000 to be exact.

CHAPTER 6

NEVER GIVE UP

Two weeks passed by and no new scholarships or grants were coming through. I was still a whopping $58,000 away from my dream school, with only a few weeks before classes began.

The week before I'd asked my friends at student aid services if they knew of any other way I could earn the rest of the money. They had no solutions for me, but wished me the best.

It seemed like I was back to square one. I was still tithing and trusting God as my source of supply but nothing seemed to be coming through. I was now really starting to give up the fight. Then one day, I did.

With only 3 weeks remaining, I came home to my apartment and realized my time was up. My friends were all registered for their classes, the University athletic programs were beginning pre-season within a few days and I was completely left in the dust. It was at this time I realized the school year would start without me. My dream was over. So I finally gave up the fight.

I remember very clearly the exact time I decided I was completely defeated. I was on my way to the mailbox before heading upstairs to my apartment. Rather than the typical excitement to see if there was a scholarship waiting for me in the mail, I said to myself, "I bet there's nothing good in here for me."

I'd given up the fight to believe that God was my unlimited source of supply. I had given up the fight to believe that God could do the impossible. I had forgot that my God can raise something that is dead back to life. I had forgot that with Him *there is always hope.*

Although I had conceded defeat and literally spoke it into being, immediately after I said those words I knew in my heart that the statement wasn't true. Realizing this, I decided right then to muster up every ounce of faith in my soul, body, mind and spirit. I stood in front of that stupid mailbox and declared with authority, "There's a scholarship in this mailbox for me from BGSU for $4,000 and it's mine!"

I quickly opened up the mailbox, grabbed the letters inside and ran straight upstairs to open them in my apartment. When I opened the door I saw my roommate and his girlfriend sitting on the couch. So I sat in between them, found one letter from BGSU in the pile, held it up in the air and declared with the same authority, "This letter is a scholarship from BGSU for $4,000 and it's mine!"

They were *completely blown away* and they began to congratulate me with their words and overwhelming hugs. I had to break the news to them that I hadn't opened any of the letters yet. Needless to say, they thought I was a little bit nutty.

I opened the letter with them and I pulled out a pamphlet with a sticky note on it. It was from the lady in student aid services and it read, "Ryan this just passed by my desk, I've never seen this scholarship before but I thought it would be perfect for you."

Turns out it was a scholarship *tailor made* for me. It allowed me to volunteer anywhere I wanted in the United States for a total of 60 hours in the spring semester (which was perfect for me as a student athlete because spring was my off-season and I had more time to commit to extracurricular activities). And just for fun, guess what the scholarship amount was for? $4,000 on the nose! That's right! Praise God!

I ended up making the application deadline in the nick of time and was chosen to receive that scholarship for that year and my senior year for a total of $8,000.

Very shortly after this, I received a call from another dear friend I had made in the residency department. For the past year I had been working at earning in-state residency to be eligible for in-state tuition. That day her call was not to inform me that more paperwork was needed to qualify, but rather to inform me that I had received in-state tuition and my bill for college had been cut nearly in half!

It was almost too much to take in. I couldn't have imagined all this would have happened. My bill was shrinking exponentially with God in the limelight!

But God wasn't through with me yet. He knew I was still short several thousand dollars, and He also knew the desires of my heart were yet to be fulfilled in regards to my athletic career.

A few days went by and I was finally ready to settle and decide on attending Bowling Green. Although I had received better scholarship offers academically and athletically from other universities, I decided that Bowling Green fit me best according to my priorities. This meant I was going to have to call the soccer coach and concede to walk-on the soccer team.

This *did not* sit well with me considering the other athletic scholarships I was offered elsewhere. But I figured since I had a majority of school already paid for I could possibly get a good job or get another big scholarship to cover the rest of my bill. I caught myself pushing God out of the picture again. Fortunately for me, God had a grand finale of blessings prepared to show His love and power to me.

Exactly *one hour* before I was going to call the coach (and I decided to eat lunch before I was going to call and concede to walk on the soccer team), I received a phone call from him! The call was short and sweet. He said, "Ryan what do we need to get you on this team?"

I told him all that I had received in financial aid and I told him what I needed in order to have my bills paid so I could play for his team. I told him my financials were a determining factor for me, as I simply wouldn't go into debt to attend college. His response was, "That shouldn't be a problem Ryan. If you're still interested in playing for us, I'd like to welcome you as a Falcon."

I expressed that I still was interested and I hung up the phone, simultaneously raising both of my arms into the sky in victory, while slowly tearing up.

At that moment, I vowed to God that when my college career was over, I would share my testimony and learning's with others so they could see the kind of adventures that are possible to have with their heavenly Papa too.

Allow God to provide for you. He's crazy about you and He will show you His might when you put Him in the limelight. We can trust our God. He is living, real and as we partner with Him anything is possible.

CHAPTER 7

THE RIDE OF A LIFETIME

For my 18th birthday, the most exciting thing I could think to do was to jump out of an airplane. I roped my best friend Steven into going with me so I didn't feel completely nuts.

We first signed a document stating that we wouldn't sue the skydiving company if we died. We then got dressed in funny looking jumpsuits. Before we knew it we were waving goodbye to our families (hopefully not for the last time) as we took off in our small passenger plane.

One thing that really stood out to me as we climbed higher and higher in our small plane was the serenity and peace that my tandem instructor seemed to have (a tandem instructor is the person strapped to your back when you jump). He was so calm.

He read a portion of a novel and took a short nap on our ascent to 14,000 feet. He had the utmost confidence that we would arrive back to the earth safely because he had done it hundreds, if not thousands of times before.

I, on the other hand, had never jumped out of a plane before and I found myself wanting to back out. Just as I was about to throw in the towel and decide not to jump, I saw my friend Steven disappear out the side door with his instructor. Now I knew there was no turning back. If I didn't jump now my best friend would brand me as a chicken for the rest of my life. I had to jump.

As my tandem instructor and I scooted closer and closer to the door my heart began to feel like it was beating out of my chest. He held me over the ledge of the open door with 14,000 feet of open air between us and the ground and he yelled, "Lean back! Let's do a back flip!"

Although I couldn't manage to say anything, I closed my eyes, leaned back and jumped out of a perfectly good airplane into thin air.

All I could do at first was scream like a newborn baby as I experienced the unexplainable rush of my body falling at 120mph. Falling out of the sky like that felt exactly like being on a rollercoaster (multiplied by 100 or so).

As we were falling, the craziest thing happened. My tandem instructor tapped me on the head to get me to open my eyes and see the majestic sites of the Arizona mountain ranges (they were amazing to view from up here). As I was enjoying the view I began to realize that I now felt like I was floating rather than falling. The experience that was previously haunting me now became the best ride of my life. It was an unforgettable rush.

When we got back to solid ground, Steven and I immediately wanted to do it all over again. The scare of the whole experience was gone because we had done it and it was the most amazing ride we had ever been on. We're still so thankful we didn't back out or we would have missed out on that experience.

The whole student athlete college experience, for me, was similar in many ways to skydiving. I didn't really know what to expect, I was freaked out not knowing if I was going to make it, and I needed to take a leap of faith to trust that my experienced instructor would help me get to the ground safely. Because I trusted the most experienced instructor of all, God, to help me navigate the journey, I have a testimony to share that I never would have had utilizing my own strength and resources.

We must remember that God is just as powerful today as He was in Bible times. We must remember that God is able to do exceeding, abundantly above all that we can ask or think for your college experience as He did for mine.

I believe you will enjoy the ride of a lifetime in college as you place your trust in God to be a debt-free student athlete. It's certainly an adventure that you wouldn't want to back out of. In the end, I believe you'll experience the reality of God's love and power and see your "jump" with God as the only way to live.

Choose God. Let Him be your strength, recognize there is nothing too great for Him, place your trust in Him and enjoy the ride. It may be a bit scary at first but, believe me, when it's all over you will see God's great power and love for you in a very tangible way. You'll have a story to tell to the world and a way of life that only true people of faith get to experience.

Enjoy your jump! You'll be happy you did.

CHAPTER 8

IT TAKES TEAMWORK

It was summer break after my second year of college. I was super excited to be out of school to prepare and train to enter the height of my soccer career as a Division I athlete. The summer was a perfect time to train hard while showcasing my skills in some of the leagues in the city.

On a Wednesday evening, I found my first gig on a team that needed an extra player. I pictured myself scoring tons of goals and showing off my skills with my new team. That ended up *not* being the case that night.

The whistle blew and I was passed the ball. I pulled off some great moves and passed the ball to one of my teammates across the field. They lost control of the ball and the other team came charging down the opposite side of the field, working the ball down the field together beautifully and scored a goal on us within a few seconds.

We regrouped from the shocking first minute of the game and within a few minutes I got the ball again near the other team's goal and whipped in a seemingly perfect cross for one of my teammates to score, but they missed the wide-open net. Immediately after the miss, the other team charged our goal and scored yet again. The remainder of the game went just like that and we ended up losing a lot to a little.

That night I learned my ability to win a soccer game and my effectiveness as a soccer player was largely dependent on the teammates surrounding me. I realized how much I relied on my teammates throughout a game to succeed. It was clear that I simply could not win by myself.

In a similar way, you'll need the help of a great team to get your college education paid for without borrowing money. Here are the steps to develop your team of all-stars that will help you graduate debt-free.

CHAPTER 9

START WITH ONE ALLY

When I was making my second transfer to Bowling Green State University from two separate community colleges, I needed the help of many people. The team God helped me put together was astounding, but it all started with one good teammate, one ally.

The key to building your strong team is to *start with someone you trust*. If you begin building your team with a trusted ally, they will refer you to people they genuinely trust and you'll break into a vein of quality people, which in turn produces a great team. These people will turn into your team of all-stars who will help you find the money you'll need to graduate debt-free.

As I shared earlier with you in my testimony, my first trusted teammate was the coordinator of the campus Bible fellowship I attended. She referred me to someone she respected and trusted in student aid services, this man referred me to the middle-aged phantom woman that he respected and trusted, and the first result was the $2,000 grant. This grant giver then led me to a fantastic volunteer scholarship that led me to $4,000 that year *and* the following year. Those 3 teammates led me to $10,000 in scholarships and grants!

It's critical that we take time to connect with a coach, advisor, church minister, friend, boss or someone you respect and trust to begin to build a web of talented teammates. With this team you will have the support needed to graduate without borrowing money. They will show you the paths to take to get the funding you'll need to reach your goals as a debt-free student athlete. You do your best, they'll do their best, and God will do the rest.

CHAPTER 10

FOLLOW THE TRAIL OF TRUST

As you build your team follow the trail of trust they provide you and do not stop. Ask them for their valued advice; see if they can connect you to another person that they trust and respect that may be able to help you reach your goal of a debt-free college education.

Let them know what you will need to attend their school and ask if they can help you or lead you to someone who may be able to help. The trail of trust they provide will get warmer and warmer until you start meeting teammates that can help you find the money you'll need for school.

Even after college, I've continued to see the importance of having a great team in all areas of my life. It's how businesses reach new heights, how organizations accomplish great things, how families stick together, and it's how the body of Christ operates. Each member giving their all to see those around them achieve their dreams and goals.

Our goal is to get your college education fully financed with God's help, and with the team He helps you build. Simply follow the trail of trusted teammates that God connects you with and you'll build the team you need to earn money for college.

CHAPTER 11

SHOW GRATITUDE

Now that we've built a strong team of trusted allies, it's vital that we show our thankfulness for them so they know their service is making a difference.

A while back, my wife and I visited some of her family in Colorado. One evening we were watching the oldest sibling compete at a swim meet. I could tell her young brothers were getting antsy so I decided to walk around the college campus with them to see if we could find something fun to do as we waited for her turn to swim.

As we walked around the inside of the athletic facility, we ran into two areas of interest, a rock-climbing wall and an indoor track. As we walked towards both attractions it was apparent that the boys thought we were not going to be able to utilize either. They saw everything as off limits.

As we approached the rock-climbing wall, we met a young man who looked like he may be in charge (he looked the part with his collared shirt and nametag). Turns out he was in charge of the wall and the indoor track. I introduced the boys and myself and we chatted for a little bit. By simply asking him a few questions about his life, I got to know him quite well. He had a great story as to why he was at the university and I quickly became interested in what he had to say about his journey.

After our conversation, I asked if it was available for us to use the rock-climbing wall. Without hesitation, he gave us full access to both attractions.

Because I simply cared about this young man's life and what he had to say, he was excited to allow us to use the equipment that was typically off limits to those who weren't a part of the university.

My young cousins seemed taken back by this at first. I explained to them that when we care for people and love them, it is natural for them to return the kindness and extend themselves to us as well. That day my little cousins and I learned that *love activates service.*

As you build your team, keep in mind these wonderful people are inspired to serve you as you show your love and thankfulness for their help. They want to know that their life and work is making a difference. And we owe other people one very important thing right? We owe them our love. So be sure to extend it! Proverbs

16:24 tells us: "Pleasant words are as an honeycomb, sweet to the soul, and health to the bones" (KJV).

As you speak kind words and love the people on your trusted team, they will be fueled to help you attain your goal of a debt-free college tenure. So continually let these wonderful teammates of yours know that you appreciate all they're doing to help you attend their college. Bake them a cookie. Send them a card. Give them a hug even!

Do you remember the first thing the man from student aid services said to me when we met for the first time? The first thing he talked about were *the cards* that those wonderful kids before me from my home bible fellowship had given him. He kept those cards in the top drawer of his desk because he was so happy he made a difference in their lives. Always remember that you're dealing with people, not just positions.

Love activates service. As you show your genuine gratitude for your teammates, it will fuel their service to you.

The first step to graduate debt-free is to build a strong team. You start with one ally that you respect and trust and follow their trail until it leads you to the right people to help finance your education. Remember that love activates the service of your teammates. As you love them and show your thankfulness for their lives, they will naturally want to help you reach your goals as debt-free student athlete.

Chapter 12

BE SMARTER THAN THE COMPETITION

When I was 14, I took a summer course on jujitsu so I could learn some sweet ninja skills.

My instructor was a very short, petite middle-aged woman weighing in around 100 pounds. She was a very sweet lady and always had a bright smile on her face while instructing us.

I remember one particular day of sparring when I was on fire. I seemed unstoppable as I beat out all of my classmates while sparring against them. I'll admit my ego was growing fast as I began defeating students who were farther along in the martial art than I was. Once I had won my way to the top, my instructor joined in and I was up to spar against her.

To be honest with you, I didn't want to spar against her because I thought I might hurt her. But she insisted and we began to spar.

I made my first move and threw her over my hip and onto the mat. At that split second I was on top of the world — unstoppable! However, in that split second of rejoicing, she used the momentum of my hip throw to flip me over her body and slam me to the ground!

She had flipped me over on my back and pinned me within a second, my arms facing the sky, fully extended, unable to move, while she sat Indian style on my chest pinning me to the ground. I was locked down by my tiny instructor and I had no escape. She made one move and I was forced to tap out (after I yelped like a baby).

Needless to say I was extremely humbled, but I was also very enlightened. I knew my instructor wasn't stronger than I was; she was simply a smarter fighter than I was.

I correlate this learning experience to my college experience because in college I learned that I didn't have to be the best student or athlete to go through college debt-free, I just needed to be smarter than my competition to win.

This is a lesson you'll want to learn now before entering college so you don't spend your time wasting energy, getting frustrated and working overtime to get results. It's time to learn how to fight smart and win. The next chapters will show you how.

CHAPTER 13

KNOW YOUR PRIORITIES

I was up super late one night watching an infomercial on what was apparently the world's sharpest knife and scissor set. I was going to change the channel, but when I saw the scissors cut straight through a shoe, I was glued to the TV.

I'm typically not a sucker for infomercials but by the end of this one I really wanted, and felt like I needed, those knives and scissors! And of course if I ordered in the next five minutes, I'd get a second pair of scissors and the special holster case (a $200 value) absolutely free!

The media can cause us to feel like we need and want things that, in reality, we may not actually need or even want. After that infomercial wore off on my senses, I was amazed at how silly it would have been to purchase those knives. I couldn't believe I was almost hooked!

We must understand that colleges and universities are businesses, and they market through the media very well. They want you to spend your money with them. This is the reason why you will be bombarded with media of all kinds from universities all over the country and world as you approach your time to choose a college.

If you haven't already, get prepared to receive all sorts award letters with financial aid opportunities (mainly consisting of loans) along with tons of literature endeavoring to prove that "X" university is the university you really want and need to attend.

It's in this arena that you'll need to be smarter than your competition. You will combat the many marketing messages by setting your priorities to figure out what *you want*, not what the universities say you want. This point is critical so I'll repeat it. *It's vital to set your priorities to identify what you want, not what the universities say you want.*

When we get ready to choose an institution to get a higher education our mindset can tend to be backwards. We tend to shape ourselves to fit the mold of a college, university or Ivy League, when we should have the school fit our criteria and priorities.

Now is the time to write down your priorities together as a family so you can find the college that truly suits you best.

How do you do this exactly? We first figure out what's of greatest priority to you and your family. Examples may include, your spiritual growth, the education you receive, how much the college or university costs to attend, the competitiveness of the athletic program, the extracurricular activities on campus, or the schools distance from home. Whatever your priorities are, write them down, formulate a list and place them in the order of importance. It's time to prioritize your priorities.

A priority list can be as simple as a numbered list in order of priority that goes something like,

1. Spiritual Growth and Development
2. Family and Support System
3. Finances
4. Educational Program
5. Athletic Program
6. Distance from Home

Let's take some time right now to have you and your family set up a list of your priorities. This way we can get clear on what it is you need and want throughout your college tenure. You may find it helpful to get more specific with bullet points under each topic to clarify what is meant.

Remember, God says in Psalm 37:4 that as we delight in Him, He will give us the desires of our heart. With that in mind, it may be wise to put Him first on our priority list, and then put down all the desires of your heart after Him. As we delight in our heavenly Father, He gives us our desires. We can rest in His promise.

<u>Our Priorities for College</u>

1.

    •

    •

2.

    •

    •

3.

    •

    •

4.

    •

    •

5.

    •

    •

Now that you've set and agreed upon your priorities as a family, you can focus on the schools that fit *your desires and priorities*, not schools that want you to fit their mold.

This process of evaluating and writing down your priorities will provide so much peace and clarity in your college search and will help to narrow down the schools you are truly interested in. We did this all by filtering the college media through the strainer of your priorities.

Now when a university advertisement or marketing message comes to you, you can simply filter it through your priority list.

Start with your top priority and work your way down the list to see if it suits your criteria. As you do this, your list of potential colleges and universities to attend should easily be honed down to 3-5 schools as your college search progresses.

Now that we've narrowed down your college choices to 3-5 schools, you'll have no need to spend gobs of money on recruiting services.

Because you've narrowed down your search to 3-5 schools utilizing your priorities as a filter, you can easily carry the workload to get recruited on your own. This gives you an upper hand on your recruiting competition.

College coaches love student athletes who are self-starters. They're looking for student athletes who have the initiative to contact them and are willing to work smarter and wiser to get noticed. This is the kind of player coaches want on their teams.

Several of my good friends who were very talented athletes and tremendous students, elicited the service of recruiting companies. Although it's exciting to feel like you have someone who will connect you to hundreds of schools, it costs quite a bit and is likely to be less effective than reaching out to your 3-5 schools personally.

From the experiences I have witnessed, mostly all of the young men and woman who utilized recruiting services didn't get the payoff they were looking for. They went to schools that seemed obscure, were out-of-state, and quite expensive. Although the message from the recruiting services seemed to portray that they would get you into your dream school fully financed, the financing packages ended up consisting mainly of student loans, and the dream school ended up being an obscure school.

For my friends who used these services everything seemed great until they realized that they couldn't afford school, were borrowing tons of money and didn't really have a genuine connection to their coach because their recruiting had been done through a third party. Long story short, most of them transferred to different universities with loads of debt in their wake.

Fortunately your recruiting process will be very different. Your time and energy will be concentrated on the 3-5 colleges that fit you best, you will know the in-depth details of your top picks, and you will see which school God is opening up the door for you to attend.

So pat yourself on the back and give everyone in your family a big bear hug! Together, you've set your priorities and are now on the fast track to finding the 3-5 schools that best fit your needs and desires. You will not fall prey to college media messaging, and you will have great clarity in your college search because you have filtered your choices through the priorities that you and your family have set. You're a rock star student athlete!

Chapter 14

SMART OPTIONS FOR COLLEGE

Having a variety of options is important as you search for the right school. We want to make sure we don't limit how God can work. This means we want to be open to different forms of higher education ranging from private universities to community colleges (as a side note — although in this book we are concentrating on a higher education specifically in college, we may not want to rule out the possibilities of a higher education in the realm of a trade school, seminary school, or even missions work).

Initially you may be turned off by the idea of looking into many different forms of higher education but remember this: *it's not where you go to school that matters most, it's the effort you put into the education you receive that largely determines the quality of your education.*

I know it might sound like a line, but in most cases, *you make the college experience what it is.* There are students attending the finest universities in the world, gleaning next to nothing from the education because they are not putting their energy into their studies. There are also students attending some of the most humble community colleges and less prestigious schools, but are taking home an education that we simply can't put a price tag on.

One option that can help you graduate as a debt-free student athlete is to attend a community college for your first two years.

Unless you're planning to be a doctor, architect, lawyer, or some other specialized profession, you'll need to complete the typical 1-2 years of general education courses required to graduate. Most of the time you will find that *these courses are the same wherever you take them.* Whether you go to community college or a very prestigious university, the course material and credit count toward graduation are often identical.

There are some perks to attending community college. First of all, you're more likely to receive personal attention at a community college in a class of approximately 30 or less, than at a four-year university where you may have hundreds of students in a general education course.

Another perk of going to a community college is that it gives you a new lease on your GPA life. If you were not a standout academically in high school, this is your time to shine. If you become a 4.0 student in community college, it's likely your new record will become the focal point for admission at your future four-year university.

Generally, it's easier to attain an athletic or academic scholarship at a community college. Athletically, due to the quick two-year turn around for athletes, it's likely that coaches have a healthy amount of athletic scholarships available each year. Academic scholarships are also more likely to be attained at a community college because these institutions value having quality students representing their community college. They desire student athletes like you!

One of the final perks to attending a community college: *You will pay a fraction of the price for the same general education courses you will take at a four-year university.*

For those who do decide to go the community college route, here are some big tips for you ...

1. Make sure your community college credits transfer to the top 3-5 universities you are interested in transferring to after community college. Work closely with the transfer evaluation services department at those universities, so you don't waste your time in classes that do not transfer credit for credit. You'll want to be on track in your course studies when you get to a four-year university, not behind.

2. If your sites are set on a four-year university that is out-of-state after community college, you may consider using your second year of NJCAA athletic eligibility and transfer to a community college in the state of that university to establish in-state residency for the following year. In many cases this can cut your tuition in half, if not more. This is something that I did, and it's very attainable, but check with your trusted teammates in the residency department of the university to get details on this to ensure that you meet that states specific residency requirements.

Because my number one choice BGSU didn't have the funding for me to attend my sophomore year of college, I transferred from a community college in Arizona, to a community college just 20 minutes from the campus of BGSU.

I simply emailed the coach my student athlete profile and he ended up offering me a full athletic scholarship, which paid for my out-of-state tuition in full. So that year I completed the remainder of my general education courses, and didn't pay a penny to do it, all while establishing in-state residency for the following year at my number one four-year university choice.

As I stated earlier, it does tend to be easier to attain athletic and academic scholarships at community colleges. After my first two years of community college, I had been paid over and above my tuition and fees by a total of $3,000. You know where that money went? Straight into my bank account to be used for any college expenses in the future. Not a bad start!

Before we close this section on community colleges, I'd like to address a myth in the arena of community college athletics.

For some reason, there's a myth that playing your sport at the community college level is somewhat distasteful as an athlete. This could not be further from the truth. Several community colleges I know have athletic programs that constantly compete against heavy-hitting Division I and Division II universities. If you play for a good community college you will see that they can really hold their own.

During my time at community college, I played with and against soccer players who have played professionally, are current professionals and some who are considered some of best soccer players in the world. Young men I played against in community college, I have watched play on TV in the largest sporting event in the world — The World Cup. Even I have had the honor to play soccer professionally in the United States after I graduated.

State universities are wonderful as well. They tend to be less expensive for in-state residents. Going to these universities allows you to live far enough away from home to have your own space, but close enough to enjoy a great home-cooked meal and the love of your family when you need it most. As you'll see when you go off to school, home cooked meals and the love of your family are two things you'll grow to appreciate more and more.

Ivy League and private schools can be deceiving financially. Although it's typical to perceive they are super expensive, there are Ivy Leagues and private schools that will financially support a majority of your tuition and fees if you get accepted. A recent interview I had with the admissions director at a top Ivy League school proved to me how a $63,000 per year tab quickly becomes an very average $23,000 per year tab, once grant and scholarship aid from the school is distributed. The toughest part is actually getting into a school with a six percent acceptance rate. Point being, it's a good idea to make sure you know your financial aid details before you count out Ivy League and private schools.

My aim in this section is to encourage you to not limit yourself or God with your college choices. You can have an amazing college tenure no matter where you go to school.

So keep your options open. Feel free to have a wide variety of options ranging from community colleges to private institutions if you see fit. This way we don't limit God or ourselves in the process. He has the best in store for us!

CHAPTER 15

SMART SCHOLARSHIPS

Are you passionate about your family heritage? There are grants and scholarships for that. Are you in the military? There are grants and scholarships for that. Were your parents or grandparents in the military? There are grants and scholarships for that. Are you a Mayflower descendent? There are grants and scholarships for that. Are you passionate about volunteer work? There are tons of grants and scholarships for that. Do you own a really cool duck stamp collection? You guessed it; there are even grants and scholarships for that!

Grant and scholarship money is out there! The trick to winning these awards is to *apply to scholarships and grants that are unique to you, and ones that you are passionate about.*

My wife studied abroad in France for a semester, which tacked on an additional semester for her to graduate. Her full-tuition leadership scholarship ended after four years so she needed to come up with one semester's tuition. She decided to apply for a scholarship for seniors committed to serving the public. Although it was great that this award was the highest paying scholarship on campus, it required the applicants to be a full-time student for the following year. Although she didn't fit the scholarship requirements perfectly she applied because the scholarship was unique to her and she was passionate about its mission.

In her application, she wrote an additional note explaining her reason for applying even though she didn't meet all the requirements for the award. Sure enough, it was this note that caught the scholarship panel's eye. The panel could see that Stephanie was truly passionate about serving the public with the education she had received. Because the purpose and mission of the scholarship was to help these kind of graduating seniors launch forward into the world to help serve the public she was awarded the scholarship! In addition to her winning the award, Steph, her parents and I all got to have lunch with the president of the university!

The key to winning scholarships and grants is to apply to ones that are unique to you and ones that you're passionate about. Your passion for the matter will come out in your essay and increase your odds drastically of winning the award. We don't want to fill out a scholarship because it's worth $25,000. We apply for scholarships that we're passionate about, that are unique to us, and we win.

An important note is to remember that the grant and scholarship committees want to be *moved* by your essay. They want to hear *why and how the specific topic of the scholarship has shaped your life.*

When writing scholarship and grant essays keep the focus on yourself rather than others. The committee wants to have an idea of the person you are and how the subject matter has impacted your life. Your essay is the best way for them to get to know you without being face to face with them. Give them insight into your life and share why the message of their scholarship is important to you.

Winning grants and scholarships to graduate debt-free, requires a shift in our thinking to apply only for the awards that are unique to us, and ones that we are passionate about. When we see the scholarship or grant is tailor made for us, we apply, write an essay from our heart, and win.

Winning grants and scholarships is such an effective way to pay for school. You may win some and you may not win some but keep in mind that the hours you spend on the scholarship divided into the award amount often equals out to a great hourly wage. If you spend ten hours on a small $1,000 scholarship and win it you just worked for $100/hr. Not too shabby! If you don't win, the worst that can happen is that you spent those hours honing your ability to effectively communicate through your writing which will impact the next scholarship or grant you apply for.

Where can you find these grants and scholarships? There are plenty of websites that can help you hone in on specific scholarships like Fastweb.com. However, some of the best people to ask are college admission counselors. They know the ropes and are up-to-date on the latest scholarships and grants that you can apply for. It would be of great benefit to visit a college or university near you and make a friend in the admissions, financial aid, or student aid services department to help you get ahead in this arena.

Finding scholarships and grants that are unique to you will help narrow your field of competition. Getting passionate about the topic helps you stand out from your competition.

Go, Fight, Win!

CHAPTER 16

THE FAFSA

There are only a few things we need to understand about the FAFSA that will help us graduate debt-free.

The two things the FASFA can provide that are not loan related are ...

1. The Pell Grant
   If your family's financial need is relatively high you could receive a Pell Grant. There are several other factors involved that affect the award amount beyond financial need such as, cost of attendance for the college or university, enrollment status and how many terms you're enrolled in. The average Pell Grant recipient in 2012-13 received $3,477.

2. Work-Study

   Work-Study is a great program where you can work
   a job related to your field of study and not be charged
   tax on the money you earn. If you are granted a
   Work-Study opportunity from FAFSA and you need
   the finances I highly recommend this program.

It's important to recognize that you shouldn't *rely on the FAFSA
to finance your education.* The FASFA will offer you many forms
of "financial aid" but it's very likely to be in the form of student
loans. Unless your family qualifies as being in financial need, you
will not receive an overwhelming amount money in the form of
grant aid but rather in the form of student loans.

One piece of advice I would share on the FAFSA is to consider
hiring someone to fill it out for you. You may find that your
accountant or financial advisor could help you with this task. The
FAFSA form can be quite a headache to fill out, and you could
save your valuable time and peace of mind by having someone else
fill out these forms for you. If you have a professional fill it out,
you can be sure that the information is accurate and you'll save
yourself many hours of potential frustration and anxiety.

The overall message with FASFA is that we shouldn't bank on it
to fit the bill for college. You'll *need* to fill it out to see if you are
eligible for the Pell Grant and Work-Study program and because
it's a requirement to apply for most other grants and scholarships.

So plan ahead and make sure you complete your FAFSA as soon as
you're able to. Once you have it filled out and behind you, believe
for the best, enjoy receiving the Work-Study and Pell Grant if
you're awarded it, and keep moving ahead. We've got some more
work to do!

CHAPTER 17

THINK OUTSIDE THE BOX

I had never seen anything like it! We were in the middle of the second half of a grueling soccer match, tied 0-0 against a nationally ranked team, when the ball went out of bounds for a throw in. A teammate of mine quickly picked up the ball, took a few steps back and threw the ball in from the sideline by doing a front handspring! I was stunned as the ball flew nearly 40 yards straight at the goal, went off the goalie's hand and into the back of the net to put us in the lead! Because my teammate thought outside the box, we won!

Thinking outside the box can lead us to great success in college as well. Here's some ways to think outside the box throughout college. These tips saved me tens of thousands of dollars during my college tenure. I believe they will save you some big bucks too.

1. Live Off-Campus and Buy Your Own Groceries
   It cost me half as much money to live off campus as it did on campus. This was the difference of several thousand dollars every semester. This is one advantage of coming to a university as a transfer student from a community college because many universities only allow you to live off-campus in your junior and senior years of college.

2. Inquire About Grants at the School
   Remember the $2,000 Excellence Grant that I received? I wasn't the only person that year who received that grant. I have several other friends who also received grants from the university for $1,000 and more by simply taking a stand to live debt-free throughout college. They were awarded those finances because they *stood their ground*. Some of my friends who couldn't afford to pay their bill upfront were given a special payment program so they could pay their bill in small chunks over time with no interest.

3. Use the Work-Study Program from the FASFA to Do Your Homework While Making a Tax-Free Paycheck
   If you're a student athlete, it's likely your coach knows a place for you to get a job on campus where your duties may be something minimal like checking people into a gym, monitoring a front desk, or some other occupation that's necessary but requires less engagement while working. It's possible to get a job on campus where you can actually get your homework done while earning a tax-free paycheck! As a side note, depending on

your Work-Study coordinator, it can be pretty easy to get a job doing just about anything, especially if you're in the first two years of college taking your general education courses. The more specified you get in your field the stricter the regulations are for your Work-Study job to get approved. For example, if you're studying pre-med it might be harder to swing a Work-Study job as a waitress and get it approved (seeing that your Work-Study job is to be related to your field of study).

4. Consider Becoming a Resident Advisor
    Being an RA typically gets you free, or drastically reduced, room and board on campus, as you oversee a hallway of students on your floor. If you're good with people, are responsible, and enjoy meeting new folks, then this can be a great way to eliminate or drastically decrease your room and board fees. Be sure to check into the program requirements first to get the details of what's required on your part because as a student athlete it's likely you'll be training or traveling with your team quite often.

5. Textbooks Tips
    Books can cost over $1,000 per semester. If you want this cost taken care of, first ask your coach. Many times you'll find that they have book scholarships available. You can also look specifically into book scholarships on campus and apply for them.

    You may want to check for your textbooks online (just make sure you have the correct ISBN number for the book you will need).

Another great idea is to check your college library for your course books as soon as you know what book is required for the class – by doing this you could get your textbooks for just a few dollars! Many times if your university library doesn't carry the textbook you need, they can order it from another university library that does. All you'll pay is the shipping cost.

If all else fails, you could also consider sharing the book with a classmate or friend who is in the class. You both pay half of the cost for the book and share it throughout the semester.

6. Transportation Tips

You'll probably get around campus and town faster and way easier with a bike, rollerblades, long-board, scooter or something with a motor under 5 horsepower. If you don't absolutely need a car, I wouldn't recommend bringing one to college. You'll be paying for gas, insurance and even a parking pass. It's likely that you'll be able to get a ride from your circle of friends and shuttle services are a very common and effective way to travel on and off campus.

I brought a car to school, and I ended up being the chauffer for many people. At times I wished that I was on the other end of that bargain (although it was fun to give the gift of a ride to my friends sometimes).

We've learned that we don't have to be the best student or athlete to get through college debt-free. We just need to compete smarter than our competition to win. As debt-free student athletes we will have to work smarter to have our education fully funded.

We now have established our priorities to choose the right school for us, we are able to filter the college media, we are putting our concentrated effort into 3-5 diverse schools that match our priorities and we are pursuing them, putting our best foot forward.

By working smarter than your competition and thinking outside the box, you'll enjoy the freedom of financial liberty during and after college. Enjoy!

CHAPTER 18

GETTING RECRUITED

I was not born with a natural gift for my sport. When I was around twelve years old, I was affectionately called the Pillsbury Doughboy by my mom, which spread like wildfire amongst our family.

Even though I so badly wanted to be like my cousins and uncles who were great college athletes and coaches, I knew I wasn't even close to their level of skill. That was until one summer when I put some concentrated effort into being the best soccer player I could be.

That summer during the day you would find me doing three things — working out, running, or playing in soccer games. That summer of intense drive and focus changed me as an athlete and soccer player as I entered tryouts in the fall. My friends wondered what had happened to me. I was faster, stronger, and I actually had skill! I really turned some heads. With the same effort throughout the seasons, my improvements continued. From this experience I learned that focus and a strong work ethic were pivotal to succeed in my sport.

Years later after being recruited as a Division I athlete I realized it took the same focus and strong work ethic to get recruited. In order to be recruited to play your sport in college, you too will need to have a strong work ethic and focus to reach your goals.

In this section we'll learn how to concentrate our efforts to sell ourselves to college coaches and be the best recruits we can be. In the same way it took diligent effort for you to become skilled at your sport, it will take diligent effort to get recruited and to get the athletic scholarship you want from your college coach.

To start out, we must recognize that unless you're dunking at age 10, or doing something spectacular in your sport, it's unlikely that coaches are going to come knocking at your door. You will have to *sell yourself to them* and put in the work to get noticed by coaches.

To do this efficiently, you will want to first concentrate your efforts to the 3-5 schools you are interested in attending. This allows you to put your best foot forward with the schools that you want to attend and make a strong impression on the coaches there.

Here are some ideas to help sell yourself the best way possible. Put in the work here and favorable results are sure to follow.

1. Make a Strong Recruiting Video
   This video should be short and sweet. It should be a powerful 3- to 7-minute video that reflects your ability, and who you are as a student athlete with great quality. It should paint an honest picture of who you are and what you can do. Coaches want to see you showcase your skill in the video, so do some things that show you're fundamentally sound in your sport. Show some flair and provide some quality game footage.

   I will say if the video is over 7 minutes, you'd better be *really* good. These coaches value their time and the more efficient your video is the more likely they will be to be interested in you. Imagine if you were a coach and had hundreds of athletes sending you videos to watch. You would probably get to the point where you could watch a few minutes and get all you needed from the video. That's exactly what many coaches do. I've heard coaches say that they can assess their interest in an athlete within a minute or so of watching most recruiting videos.

   Your recruiting video may be your first impression so keep it short, powerful, and showcase yourself the best you can. Coaches will be impressed with this kind of a video.

   Make sure you are being honest in what you portray in the video. The coach will come and watch you play, so be prepared to show that same quality or better when they come to watch you.

There's no need to take 25 shots and put the one shot in the video that was perfect. Allow the video to portray your playing ability accurately.

This all being said, if you feel you can produce a good quality video as stated above, that's wonderful! If you're not sure, have a professional do it so it comes out in good taste and shows you pay attention to detail. Remember the quality of your video will portray to the coaches the kind of person, student, and athlete you are. So strut your stuff! You're sons and daughters of God!

2. Develop a Student Athlete Profile
    Student athlete profiles are easy to make and can be made on Microsoft Word or through websites online. There are ways you can simply send a link to a coach in an email so he can check your profile online if he desires. It's a good idea to send the coach a paper copy as well.

    Your student athlete profile should give the coach an overall perspective of the kind of person, student and athlete you are. Include things such as your contact information, GPA, SAT and ACT scores, extra curricular activities, community service, academic honors, and athletic references and their contact information (be sure to ask your coaches if it's okay to use them as a reference *beforehand* so they are prepared when a college coach reaches out to them).

You may also want to put your anticipated major if you know it, your athletic profile, height, weight, position and achievements in your sport. Do your best to provide your best achievements. Great achievements like winning a national championship show you are used to being on a winning team and are likely to have good skill but even achievements such as being a starter, show that you are out to play and not sit the bench. Be confident of your achievements and pull out the best to share with your future coach.

While developing your student athlete profile (and while applying for scholarships and grants), remember that *any work you perform without getting paid is volunteer work*. Be sure to count your hours and put it in your profile.

3. Highlight Yourself
   STANDING OUT requires doing things so coaches remember who you are. Send your recruiting highlight video in a sharp, custom made envelope, put a nice picture of yourself on your student athlete profile, have your references call the coaches office to recommend you and help you open up the conversation about your interest in their program and school. It's important to do things that will show your creativity and ingenuity as a person, which coaches know often translates to your playing ability as well.

There is no benefit in being one-dimensional. When capturing the attention of a college coach approach it with the mindset that *the quality of your life will show in the quality of your work.* We must understand that coaches are like artists in their field. They will notice your efforts. Show them that you want to compete.

Although getting recruited and noticed by coaches is fun, there are rules that you should know about too. You should be aware of NCAA Clearinghouse rules and regulations. If you plan to possibly attend an NCAA Division I, II or III school it's important to get educated on this topic. Although there are rules and regulations involved in the recruiting process, we should be aware of them, not afraid of them. The website for the NCAA Clearinghouse will have all the information you need to register and get started. Visit www.eligibilitycenter.org for more information.

Amongst other things, NCAA Clearinghouse prevents any shady business from taking place amongst student athletes and coaches during the recruiting process. So go to the website and get informed on NCAA Clearinghouse rules and regulations so you can fully enjoy the experience of being recruited.

CHAPTER 19

THE FOLLOW-UP

Now that the coaches at your top schools know who you are and what you can do on video and on paper, it's time to get them out to see you play in a game.

You can do this by informing the head coach and assistant coaches by email or phone. Let them know where your games and tournaments will be for the upcoming season (it's a good idea to contact them before the tournaments and games that you feel would be good for them to see) and ask if they would be able to make it to any of your matches. If the coach is interested, they or their assistants will make a trip to see you play. If the coaches are interested in you they could offer to bring you to their school for an official visit (which means they pay for all, or some, of the expenses of your trip) or unofficial visit (which means it's a visit that you pay for). Keep in mind that although you can make an unlimited number of unofficial visits, you can only make five official visits due to NCAA recruiting regulations, so use them wisely. For more information on recruiting rules and regulations for NCAA divisions I, II and III visit, www.ncaa.org, for Junior College visit, www.njcaa.org, and for NAIA visit, www.naia.org.

Whether the coaches come out to see you play or they have you in for a visit simply play your best. Be yourself in every way. Be respectful and thankful for the coach's interest in you. If you visit the school, one of the coach's main concerns is to see how you meld with the team. There's no need to try and be the big man or woman on campus. The coach wants to know how well your personality will mix with the team and with the coaching staff in addition to your skill as an athlete.

Finally, when it comes time to play, be yourself, play your heart out, play with respect for those around you and have some fun while you're at it. In the end you want to find the school and the athletic program that's right for you. So enjoy your time being recruited and enjoy finding your perfect fit.

CHAPTER 20

YOUR SCHOLARSHIP OFFER

After you and the coach get a good look at each other you can begin to discuss the idea of you playing on the team. During this conversation it's appropriate to discuss financial need and athletic scholarship opportunities.

Receiving an athletic scholarship will likely be a negotiation process, not an immediate decision. If a coach seems to force you to make an immediate decision, they probably aren't looking out for your best interests. Just like the infomercial incident I shared earlier, it probably isn't a great decision to make if you are forced to make it on the spot. Be sure to discuss everything you speak to coach about with your parents before any commitments are made or any papers are signed.

At this time, you'll be offered something financially, or not, by the coach. The coach may lay down some of their cards on the table. You can feel free to be candid and honest and lay out your whole hand. You have no need to be dishonest with them, and they'll appreciate your straightforward approach. You can rest assured that they will know where you stand and will know exactly what you need in order to attend their school and play for their team.

During this time be sure to pray together as a family to see your needs come to pass. Pray for the coach to make the very best decision that will give you clarity, direction and guidance to move ahead with confidence. We know that as we delight in the Lord, He will give us the desires of our heart. Since we do delight in God we don't have to settle for less than the desires of our heart, which includes a fully funded college education.

If you are having trouble in this last stage, don't allow the coach to give up on you. Stay in touch with him or her respectfully (not desperately) to get a clear answer. Even if they decide they have no athletic funds to give, it's likely they do have many other ways to help you finance your education whether it be through book scholarships, alumni scholarship funds or even a Work-Study job position on campus.

How a coach treats you during this process is oftentimes a sign of things to come in the future. If they don't project adequate interest and they're not respectful to your desires to graduate as a debt-free student athlete that's a great sign that this college may not be the best fit for you. However, if they treat you respectfully and do their best to help you get your education fully financed that's a great sign that you may be in the right place.

Receiving an athletic scholarship is a negotiation process and won't be completed overnight, but when your needs are completely met, and you find the right college home for you, sign on the dotted line, wrap everything up, and get ready to walk the walk.

CHAPTER 21

HOW TO INCREASE YOUR ATHLETIC SCHOLARSHIP

One of the best ways to secure and increase your athletic scholarship is to put on the mind of Christ. When you are humble, work heartily and go above and beyond your call of duty for the benefit of the team, your worth *skyrockets*.

I had a John Wooden quote stuck to my locker that my girlfriend's father gave me. It said, "A player that makes a team great, is more valuable than a great player."

If you make your team better by your contribution on and off the field, court or pool, you will be of great value to your team. The result of this will be an increase of your chance of securing and attaining a greater athletic scholarship the following year.

As you'll come to see, many coaches recruit with attitude and character in mind. Great coaches understand that a player that makes their team great *is,* many times, more valuable than a great player. Your attitude and character will reflect whether this statement is true in you.

Your character and your playing ability will affect the amount of scholarship money that coach will allocate to you. But what kind of character is good character? As Christians, we're fortunate enough to have the greatest example of good character ever known and it's found in the life of our Lord Jesus Christ. 1 Corinthians 2:16 tells us that as spiritual men and women we have the mind of Christ. All we need to do is put on this mindset and continue to learn and act out Jesus Christ's example on and off the field.

Christ's mindset was one of love and sacrifice. He died for us so we could have life abundantly as John 10:10 states. Can you sacrifice yourself for the team? Can you stay after practice and work on your game? Can you swallow your pride and respect your most unlovable teammate? Can you respect the decisions your coaches make? Can you compliment your teammates when they are doing a great job or are in need of encouragement? Can you organize a spaghetti dinner with the captains of your team? Can you handle conflict with love and grace? Can you look for powerful ways to love and sacrifice for your team?

Because I operated a Christian clothing company during college I offered to make hoodies and t-shirts for the team. It was such a blast and everyone became closer because of it. Seeing our teammates walking around campus in our gear identified us as a team and we became more unified.

When we put on the mind of Christ, we will want to sacrifice for our team. This mindset will increase your worth to the team and help you secure, and possibly increase, your athletic scholarship for the future.

In order to earn an athletic scholarship we put faithful effort into the recruiting process. Getting recruited and getting athletic aid from your college coach takes concentrated effort. When your quality of work and playing ability reflects the Christ within you, you will stand out from the crowd. As you showcase your strengths and your faithful effort to do your best your coach will come to respect you and see that you are worthy to receive an athletic scholarship.

Enjoy the recruiting process and enjoy reaping the fruit of your labor as an athlete. It's a very fun ride and worth all the effort.

CHAPTER 22

BE AN AMBASSADOR

As a student athlete you will be one of the select few people on campus where nearly everyone recognizes you by face and maybe even by name. You'll be somewhat of a local celebrity on campus.

Being a student athlete in college is such an amazing opportunity to shine for God and to be a witness for Him. You will have the opportunity to use your influence for good and to share with others the great things God has done for you. It's during this special time that we can bring glory to the One who got us here!

You can look for opportunities to glorify God and be His hands and feet on your campus. As you enjoy what God has blessed you with consider utilizing your influence to glorify your heavenly Father who loves you tons.

CHAPTER 23

VICTORY

My time as a college athlete ended on a beautiful spring night —
months after our last game. Over 400 student athletes, faculty,
coaches, family, friends, teachers and alumni from BGSU,
gathered together in the student union ballroom to celebrate the
end of the year Student Athlete Award Banquet.

The purpose of the award banquet was to recognize and award
the top athletes at the university and to celebrate all the victories
that our teams had at the NCAA Division I level. The evening
culminated with the highest award, Male and Female Senior
Scholar-Athlete of the Year. To my surprise I had been nominated
for this award.

As the awards were distributed anticipation grew to know who would be chosen for the final award.

When they announced the final name of the evening for the Male Senior Scholar-Athlete of the Year my name was called. The ballroom erupted in applause. But the interesting thing was — I wasn't there. I found out I had won later that evening through a barrage of voicemails and text messages that were sent to me right after the announcement.

I really did want to be there. My athletic career had led up to that event. But earlier that year, I had made a commitment to attend a national biblical seminar called Ambassadors for Christ. Eventually, I found out it fell on the same night, at the same time.

The decision wasn't easy, but I did what had become natural to do. I remembered my priorities and God was number one. So they played a recording of me for the audience and I gave thanks to God, and the people He led me to, who gave me the opportunity to play for such a great school and athletic program.

I learned a lot that night. I realized that my heavenly Father loves me and He wants my love and relationship more than anything. I learned that as I seek Him and delight in Him, before the awards, before the sport, before my glory, He gives me all the desires of my heart and more. What a great Papa we have.

Through this book, you've been led to the fountain of living waters to enjoy relationship and partnership with God on your college journey. You've let God into the picture and cultivated an environment for the impossible to come to pass. I've also shared with you the how-to information to become a debt-free college athlete so you can come out on top when you graduate. Now it's your time to follow through on the things you learned in this book to see the miraculous results that await you in college and beyond.

Rely first and fully on God to provide for your needs. I know He won't let you down. With the Creator of the universe on your side, you will graduate completely debt-free so you can live your calling and change the world.

Enjoy every minute of your adventures with God.

He is with you.

For those of you who would like more in-depth training to graduate debt-free — I developed The Debt-Free College Athlete Academy.

In the academy you'll learn how to choose your number one school, how to get it completely paid for without needing student loans, and how to get recruited as a scholarship athlete. You'll also receive exclusive content from experts in this arena to get you the information you'll need to graduate debt-free.

If you would like for me to coach you every step of the way, I'm here for you.

Visit www.TheDebtFreeCollegeAthlete.com for more information.

For more valuable training to graduate debt-free
visit www.TheDebtFreeCollegeAthlete.com